Would You Bel e...

marzipan contains cyanide?

and other freaky **food** facts

Richard Platt

OXFORD

UNIVERSITY PRESS

Contents

OXFORD
UNIVERSITY PRESS

Great Clarendon Street, Oxford OX2 6DP

Oxford University Press is a department of the University
of Oxford. It furthers the University's objective of
excellence in research, scholarship, and education by
publishing worldwide in

Oxford   New York

Auckland   Cape Town   Dar es Salaam   Hong Kong
Karachi   Kuala Lumpur   Madrid   Melbourne
Mexico City   Nairobi   New Delhi   Shanghai
Taipei   Toronto

With offices in

Argentina   Austria   Brazil   Chile   Czech Republic
France   Greece   Guatemala   Hungary   Italy   Japan
Poland   Portugal   Singapore   South Korea   Switzerland
Thailand   Turkey   Ukraine   Vietnam

Oxford is a registered trade mark of Oxford University
Press in the UK and in certain other countries

Text copyright © Oxford University Press 2006

First published in hardcover 2006

First published in paperback 2007

British Library Cataloguing in Publication Data

Data available

ISBN: 978-0-19-911499-3

1 3 5 7 9 10 8 6 4 2

Originated by Oxford University Press

Created by BOOKWORK Ltd

Printed in China by Imago

WARNING: *The recipes and ingredients in this book are
for information only and should not be tried at home!*

Introduction

WHAT'S YOUR FAVOURITE food? Not pizza or hamburgers, surely? They are just so last year! Food can be much more interesting if you want it to be. How about tasty stir-fried locusts? Or roasted rat? Or even delicious dog stew?

In different places, people have made meals of these foods and many stranger ones. You may say "Yuck!" but there are no good reasons why we should not eat these things. After all, insects such as locusts are much like prawns, except that they don't swim in the sea. Rats in the countryside live in holes and eat vegetables, just like tasty rabbits. And are you SURE you could tell the difference between dog and chicken stew?

Most people couldn't. In fact, ask anyone who has eaten something weird and wacky what it tasted like, and they will usually answer, "Just like chicken!" In the pages that follow, you can read and wonder about the weirdness of what we eat and how we eat it. If you are tempted to taste some of the things you read about, think of this book as a collection of menus, not recipes. Many of the dishes need special preparation. Some may make you ill and some could even kill you. So if you don't know how to cook something properly, don't be tempted to try it.

Would You Believe...?

Why, how, who?
Why did zoo animals end up on the dinner table in Paris in 1871? How do tapeworms make people lose weight? Why do some people in Japan eat a fish that is deadly poisonous? Who were the first people to try hot chocolate? If you want to find out the answers, read on!

Ancient Menus

WHAT DID THE FIRST humans eat? We will never know for sure. Humans walked Earth for half a million years before anyone wrote a recipe book. But archaeologists (scientists who dig up signs of past worlds) have figured out roughly what was in these ancient people's meals.

They can tell what was on the menu thousands of years ago from gnawed bones and rubbish heaps. Occasionally, food scraps have survived in the stomachs of ancient bodies that have been preserved in mud or ice.

Would You Believe...?

Bog people
A good place to find ancient food is a bog – inside a dead body! Chemicals in bogs preserve corpses and their stomach contents for centuries. Scientists opened the gut of a 2,000-year-old body found in 1952 in a bog near Grauballe, Denmark. Inside, they found grain and weed seeds.

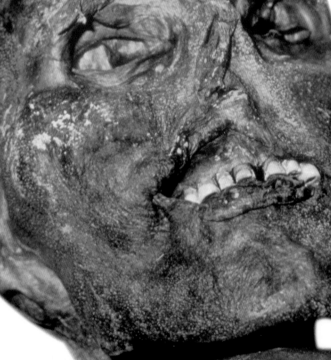

Frozen food ▲ ▶
The 4,000-year-old body of Ötzi the ice man was found in the Alps in 1991. Scientists discovered the remains of a meal of grains, red deer, ibex goat and vegetables inside his stomach.

Early humans could not choose their food. They had to eat whatever they could hunt, pick or dig up that would not poison them. Spreading out across Africa and Asia they had to change their diet as they travelled. Near the coast, they ate fish and shellfish as well as meat. And everywhere, they ate plants.

◄ ▲ Insect evidence
Bits of beetles were found in ancient human excrement in Nevada, USA.

Wild and raw
The very earliest people ate mostly raw meat. One group, which lived in a cave near Peking, China, between 700,000 and 400,000 years ago, lived mainly on deer. Scientists also found in the cave a mix of human and wild beasts' bones, but some now think that "Peking Man" was the dinner, not the diner!

▲ Wild food
Peking Man may have eaten rhinoceros and tiger as well as wild pigs and sheep.

Passing through
One way to work out what prehistoric people ate is by looking into their lavatories! Surprisingly, some of what we eat passes unchanged through our bodies. Shell, fish scales, bones, hairs, charcoal, seeds and pollen grains come out of our bodies pretty much the same as when they went in. The study of prehistoric poo even has a name – palaeoscatology. Thanks to this science, we know, for example, that the ancient people who explored Lovelock Cave in Nevada, USA, snacked on insects when they got hungry.

▲ Coprolites
Palaeoscatologists study ancient poo, which they call coprolites. Soaking coprolites in paint remover dissolves unwanted material, leaving just those vital clues to a prehistoric diet. It's hard to tell whether a coprolite comes from a human or another animal. The only sure way to find out is to look for a fossilised parasite that lives only in the human gut.

Roman Banquet

Romans reclining ▶
Romans did not sit down to eat, as we do. Instead, they lay on couches grouped around the dining table. Slaves wiped their hands for them, poured wine and brought food. They had less pleasant tasks, too.

W HEN IT CAME TO FEASTING, nobody could beat the ancient Romans. The richest of them threw huge banquets. Guests gorged themselves for hours on rich dishes. Stuffed to bursting, diners wobbled from the room to be sick. Then they staggered back to eat some more.

Roman slave chefs competed to make their masters the best food in the city. Some of the dishes they cooked, such as roast lamb, we still make today. But Romans also mixed foods in a way that we would find disgusting or just plain strange (see opposite).

Would You Believe...?

Clever cooks
Cleverness in cooking counted more than flavour in ancient Rome. Chefs made "a fish from a pig's belly, and a chicken from a knuckle of pork". They did this to show off, but also to disguise cheap ingredients. Everything was spiced with *garum*, a sauce made from fish rotted for a year.

Dormouse delicacy ▶
A favourite Roman dish was roast dormouse dipped in honey and rolled in poppy seeds. The edible dormouse is almost the size of a squirrel. It was trapped in the wild and then fattened up in a pottery jar called a *glirarium*. The dormouse sometimes grew so fat on its diet of hazelnuts and acorns that the chef had to break the jar to remove it.

● ● ● ● ● ● ● ● ● ● ● ● ● ●

ROMAN RECIPE

PORK COOKED "GARDENER STYLE"
(WITH FRESH VEGETABLES)

INGREDIENTS
Balls of minced chicken
Finely chopped roast thrushes
Little pork sausage cakes
Stoned dates
Glazed onions
Snails
Leeks
Beets
Celery
Cooked sprouts
Coriander
Whole pepper
Nuts
15 eggs

Rich pickings

The cost of eating well ruined some wealthy Romans. One greedy man paid the equivalent of £5,600 for a single, perfect fish. Another, called Apicius, spent 60 million *sesterces* (6 tonnes of gold) on banquets. When he had only 10 million left, he killed himself because he could no longer afford to live the life he enjoyed.

Fast food ▶
Only wealthy Romans ate huge meals. The poor ate mostly bread and a kind of porridge. They also bought take-away food from luncheon counters like this one preserved in the ancient town of Herculaneum in Italy.

STEP 1
Remove a pig's bones through the mouth (to avoid breaking the skin) then stuff it with all the listed ingredients.

STEP 2
Thereupon sew it tight and roast in the oven.

7

Medieval Mealtimes

MEDIEVAL DINERS certainly ate weird food. Everyone scoffed birds of all sizes. Cooks roasted swans and baked blackbirds and seagulls in pies. Strange seafood was popular too. Porpoise, known as "sea pig", was a favourite, and so were whales and seals.

You might not have recognised these beasts on the table, though. Food was often mashed in the kitchen to make it easy to eat. Instead of plates, diners ate from stale bread slices called trenchers. Cooks added costly spices to dishes to show how wealthy the host was. Meat or fish dishes shared the table with sweet, sticky puddings. Pastry cases nicknamed "coffins" contained all sorts of surprises!

▲ **Knight-shaped jug**
A jug of water was essential for rinsing greasy fingers!

The worst kitchen job was turning the meat – sometimes, a dog or goose ran in a wheel to spin the spit

Special occasions
Most food was cooked simply in huge pots, but roasted meat and fish was served whole for special occasions. Important guests looked on as carvers cut the roasts – it was all part of the entertainment.

Food with feathers ▶
To make a showy dish for banquets, medieval chefs skinned peacocks, roasted them, then put them back in their brilliant feathers for serving.

▲ Finger food
Everyone ate with their fingers, sometimes with the help of a knife or spoon. Table forks were unknown. Cooks cut up most meat in the kitchen so that diners could easily eat it with their fingers.

◀ Cool cuisine
Servants rushed from the kitchen to the table, but dishes were cold by the time they were served.

Would You Believe...?

Manners please!
Medieval table manners were very different from modern ones. Here are a few:
• Do not spit on the table. Spit politely on the floor instead.
• When you use your fingers to blow your nose, wipe them on your clothes, not the tablecloth.
• Do not belch in your neighbour's face if your breath smells.

◀ Splatting and spoiling
Each different way of cutting meat and fish was given a special name. A carver would "unbrace" a duck, "splat" a pike, "display" a crane, "fin" a chub, "barb" a lobster, "spoil" a hen and "dismember" a peacock.

Aztec Appetite

Would You Believe...? Would You Believe...?

Dog's dinner
The Mexican hairless dog, or Xoloitzquintle, is descended from dogs that the Aztecs bred for eating. Because meat was scarce, Aztec dogs were vegetarian, eating wasted food, bread and green corn. Dog flesh was a treat. Most families could afford to eat it only during festivals and celebrations.

I N 1519, SOLDIERS FROM Spain discovered ancient Mexico and its people, the Aztecs. They marvelled at the strange produce on display in a vast outdoor market in the capital city. Stalls were piled high with odd foods, all with names that sounded like rattling cutlery to European ears.

Tecuitlatl (stone dung) was a cake made from pond slime. *Atepocatl* (tadpoles), newts, frogs, white worms, ants, slugs and grasshoppers were also for sale. Most prized of all, there was *ahuauhtli* (water wheat). Spaniards brave enough to taste it said it was like crab caviar, but felt sick when they discovered that the tiny eggs were laid by the beetles we call water-boatmen.

Amazing city ▼
When Spanish soldiers first saw the Aztec's fabulous capital, Tenochtitlan, they gazed in wonder. It was built on an island in the middle of a huge lake. It was the cleanest and most beautiful city they had ever seen, and far better than even the grandest towns in Spain.

The Aztec people prized chocolate so much, they even used it as money, counting out the cacao beans like coins

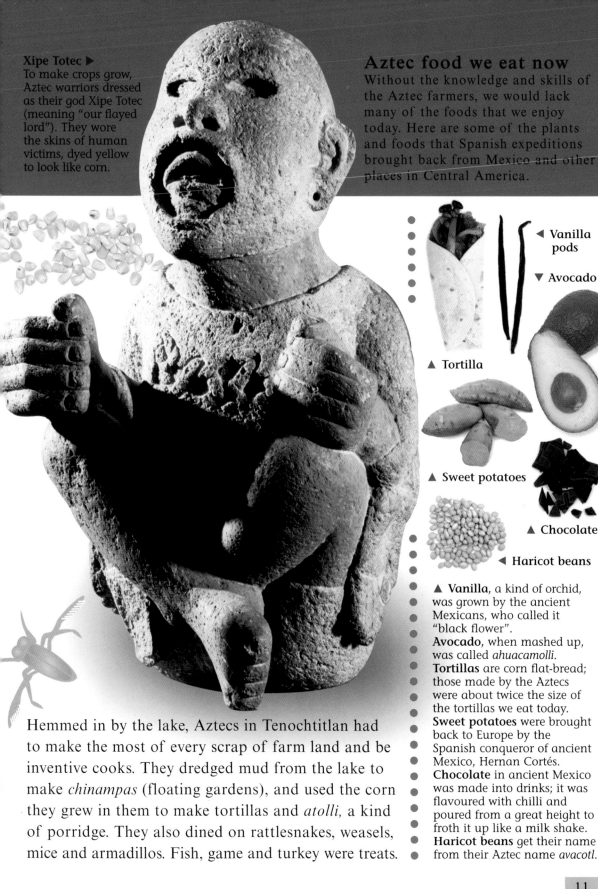

Xipe Totec ▶
To make crops grow, Aztec warriors dressed as their god Xipe Totec (meaning "our flayed lord"). They wore the skins of human victims, dyed yellow to look like corn.

Aztec food we eat now

Without the knowledge and skills of the Aztec farmers, we would lack many of the foods that we enjoy today. Here are some of the plants and foods that Spanish expeditions brought back from Mexico and other places in Central America.

◀ **Vanilla pods**

▼ **Avocado**

▲ **Tortilla**

▲ **Sweet potatoes**

▲ **Chocolate**

◀ **Haricot beans**

▲ **Vanilla**, a kind of orchid, was grown by the ancient Mexicans, who called it "black flower".
Avocado, when mashed up, was called *ahuacamolli*.
Tortillas are corn flat-bread; those made by the Aztecs were about twice the size of the tortillas we eat today.
Sweet potatoes were brought back to Europe by the Spanish conqueror of ancient Mexico, Hernan Cortés.
Chocolate in ancient Mexico was made into drinks; it was flavoured with chilli and poured from a great height to froth it up like a milk shake.
Haricot beans get their name from their Aztec name *avacotl*.

Hemmed in by the lake, Aztecs in Tenochtitlan had to make the most of every scrap of farm land and be inventive cooks. They dredged mud from the lake to make *chinampas* (floating gardens), and used the corn they grew in them to make tortillas and *atolli*, a kind of porridge. They also dined on rattlesnakes, weasels, mice and armadillos. Fish, game and turkey were treats.

Long Pig

Would You Believe...?

The raft of *Medusa*
When the French ship *Medusa* ran aground off the West African coast in 1816, 150 people escaped the wreck on a small raft. They had no food, and within days they began eating the bodies of those killed in fights. This cannibalism did not help them: just 15 were rescued.

PERHAPS THE WEIRDEST, most gruesome food that people have ever eaten is … other people. Or is it? After all, human flesh is only meat. Most of us would say "Yuck!" but in the distant past we would have been the hungry few. Cannibals (people who ate people) were common.

Archaeologists often find human bones cut by knives or cooked and cracked open, suggesting that someone ate the marrow inside. Even in recent history, there are tales of shipwreck and plane crash survivors eating their dead friends when hunger beat disgust.

▲ Patty Reed as an adult

▼ The Donner party
The most famous American cannibals were in the Donner party. This group of settlers was trapped by snow in 1846. Some of them survived by eating those who had died. Patty Reed was eight years old when she was rescued from her icy ordeal.

◄ Patty Reed's doll

▲ Scare tactics
European explorers often told stories of cannibalism among the people they conquered to make out that they were savages. This picture of the Tupinamba people of Brazil shocked 16th-century Europeans – and helped justify cruel expeditions to "civilise" them.

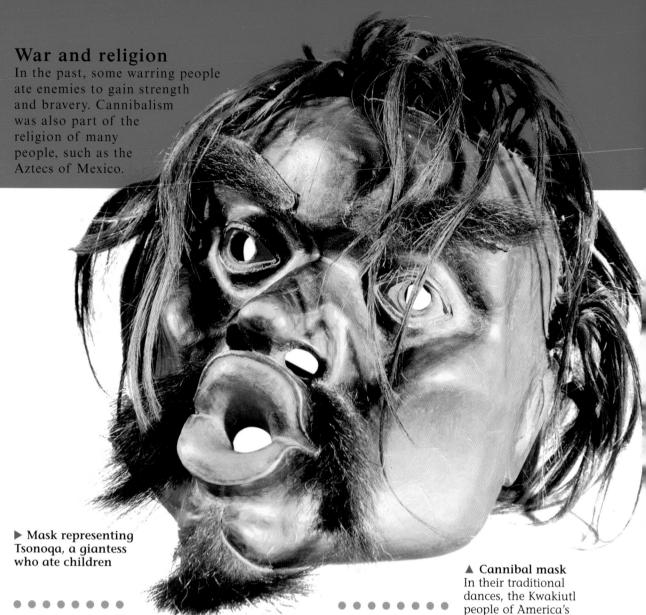

War and religion

In the past, some warring people ate enemies to gain strength and bravery. Cannibalism was also part of the religion of many people, such as the Aztecs of Mexico.

▶ Mask representing Tsonoqa, a giantess who ate children

▲ **Cannibal mask**
In their traditional dances, the Kwakiutl people of America's northwest coast wore colourful and scary masks representing cannibal characters from their legends. One dancer, wearing the mask of the Hamatsa bird monster, actually bit and ate the flesh of those watching – or was this in fact a clever conjuring trick?

It is not easy to find out what people taste like, but there's a hint from New Guinea, where human meat was called "long pig". Recipes are even harder to find. The closest thing comes from Tlaxcala in Mexico. When Spanish conquerors arrived in 1519, locals threatened to eat them. Eyewitness Bernal Diaz (1492?–1581?) knew that they weren't joking: "They had already prepared the pots with salt and peppers and tomatoes."

Some scientists believe that almost all the world's ancient people ate human flesh

Feeding on Fido

" **I** 'M SO HUNGRY I could eat a horse!" In a French restaurant, people might do just that. To many of us, eating a horse is a horrible idea, but if you were really hungry you would eat things you wouldn't touch when your stomach is full. When war cut off the food supplies in Paris in 1871, Parisian citizens ate their way through the city zoo.

▼ **Bow wow stew**
Though selling and eating dog meat is against the law in Korea, *mung-mung tang* (bow-wow stew) is on many restaurant menus there. The government cracks down on law-breakers when the nation expects many European visitors, such as in 2002 when Korea hosted soccer's World Cup.

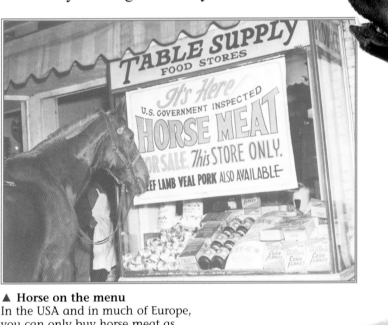

▲ **Horse on the menu**
In the USA and in much of Europe, you can only buy horse meat as dog food. In the past though, many horses ended up on the table as food for humans, as this picture of a butcher's shop in Washington, DC shows. It was taken in 1943.

The Parisians ate all the animals in the zoo **except the lions and tigers (too fierce) and the monkeys (too human)**

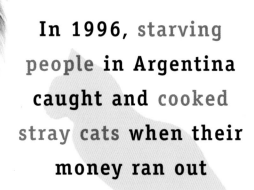

ACHAT DE CHEVAUX

Chef's cheval ▶
This hanging sign from a French butcher's shop announces proudly "horses for sale". Horse butchers in France, called *boucherie chevalines*, are less common than they once were.

The reason most of us don't eat horses, cats and dogs is probably because we keep these animals as pets. We think of them as our friends – and almost human. Few people in Asian countries have pets, and cat and dog meat is popular there. The people value animals not as companions, but for their skills – or as food.

• • • • • • • • • • • • • • • •

In 1996, starving people **in Argentina** caught and cooked stray cats **when their money ran out**

Pussy-tail stew
Some pets escape the pot because they are too useful to eat. In 1997, the Vietnam government banned restaurants in Hanoi from serving "pussy-tail stew" because mouse and rat numbers in the city had soared.

15

What if it Wriggles?

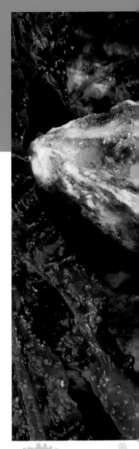

EVERYONE KNOWS FRESH FOOD IS good for you. So surely the healthiest diet of all must be living food? Diners in the world's best restaurants think so. The live oysters they eat squirm when soaked in lemon juice, and the lobsters are almost as unlucky. Restaurants keep them alive in aquariums, then cook them by plunging them, still alive, into boiling water.

◀ The human aquarium
Mac Norton, "the human aquarium", delighted European audiences in the early 19th century by swallowing live frogs and goldfish. He could also squirt water from his mouth into a bucket 6 m (20 ft) away.

CIRCUS BUSCH
Die Sensation:
Der unersättliche
MAC NORTON
Das menschliche
Aquarium

Oysters and lobsters are common dishes in Europe and the USA. To eat a wider variety of live seafood you need to travel to Asia. In Japan, such dishes have a special name: *odori-gui* (dancing food). The name describes what it does on your plate – and in your mouth! The most popular "dancing" dishes are *kuruma-ebi* shrimps and *shirouo*: the tiny fish we call whitebait. They are served swimming in a bowl. You eat them with soup, vinegar and soy sauce.

Eating an animal alive may seem cruel, but is it much less cruel to kill it first, then eat it?

Cruelty to animals?

A wriggling, dancing lunch may seem like a good advert for turning vegetarian. But those who eat live seafood say there is no cruelty in the meals. Experts claim that "shellfish and fish don't have the brains to recognise pain". Not everyone agrees!

Army survival manuals
recommend eating grubs live
and wriggling

Would You Believe...? Would You Believe...?

Monkey myth
The most famous "live food" story suggested that some Chinese diners used to cut open the heads of live monkeys and eat their brains with spoons. The story was almost certainly untrue and may have been told to make people dislike foreigners, because it was a horrifying idea.

Wriggling whitebait ▲
A tourist brochure from Japan describes this dish of *shirouo* as being a seasonal delicacy "... delicious eaten raw as *odori-gui*. When we see the weirs for catching whitebait being set in the Nonai river, we know spring has finally come."

Food
Taboos

I T CAN BE HARD TO choose food for a dinner party if your friends are religious. Hindus won't touch beef; Muslims and Jews don't eat pork. If the party is on a Friday, strict Christians will refuse to eat meat, so better serve fish – but not shellfish, because Jews won't touch that either.

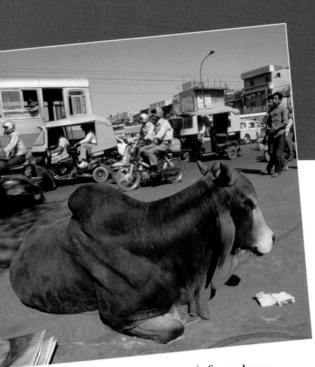

▲ **Sacred cow**
Indian Hindus will not eat beef and they cherish their cattle. In Delhi, India's second largest city, 33,000 cattle roam free. They may seem useless, but most are important to the poor farmers who own them. They cost almost nothing to feed; oxen are cheaper and better for ploughing than tractors; and cows provide vital milk.

Why do people choose their food according to how they worship? Some religious food bans can seem odd. They made more sense when they started long ago. Then many banned foods were scarce so they were often too costly to eat.

● ●

Hungry Christians cheated the Friday meat ban with help from the barnacle goose

Fish or fowl? ▶
In the Middle Ages (5th–15th centuries), everyone thought that the barnacle goose hatched from a barnacle (a kind of shellfish), so it didn't count as meat. It was therefore on many a Friday menu in Christian households.

Beating the ban
Eating insects is outlawed in the Old Testament of the Bible – a book that is sacred to both Jews and Christians. However, there is an exception: it's OK to eat locusts (see page 32). This may be because huge swarms of locusts ate crops, causing famine. If you can't beat them, eat them!

Would You Believe...? Would You Believe...? Would You Believe...?

No place for pigs

Some religious food bans may have started because of the environment or to protect people from illness. It's no surprise that Muslims and Jews don't eat pork, because keeping pigs in the Middle East, where both their religions began, used up scarce resources that humans needed.

Unclean pigs ▶
Under Jewish food rules, the pig is an unclean animal and is not kosher (good to eat). This rule may have started because pork sometimes contains tiny worms that can make you ill if the meat is not cooked properly.

Preventing poisoning ▶
Shellfish is banned under Jewish food rules. This may be because it contains poisons, and would also have spoiled quickly in the heat of the Middle East.

Religious food bans have one great advantage. By sticking to them, people gain a sense of belonging. Missing out on a food is something they share with everyone of the same faith. It brings people together and makes their faith stronger.

19

A lot of old Offal

Jelly babies ▶
If you eat a pig's trotter (foot), its sticky chewiness may remind you of jelly babies. That's because pig and cow feet are boiled up to extract gelatine – a vital ingredient in wobbly jellies and many sweets.

ARE ANY BITS OF AN ANIMAL actually impossible to eat? Not many! Butchers used to boast that when they slaughtered a pig, all they wasted was the "oink". Today, things are different. Most meat counters sell only the lean, muscular parts of animals.

The rest of the animal, called offal or "variety meat", is hard to find. It turns up on the menu in some swanky restaurants – and in some of the cheapest. If the thought of chewing on an animal's foot, ear or tail makes you gag, read no further. But offal can be delicious. Indeed, you may eat it more often than you realise.

Hidden offal

Offal is usually hard to find in supermarkets, but it is not thrown away. It is used up in all kinds of processed meat products, especially in cheap pies and sausages. To find out more, turn to pages 40–41.

▲ Ox or beef?
At the butchers, a bull gets two names. The better cuts are beef, but the offal is ox – such as ox-tail. The meat has two different names because Britons once spoke two languages. The wealthy spoke French and called what they ate *boeuf*. The poor ate the left-overs and used the English word: ox.

Would You Believe...?

Too much of a good thing
Offal, and particularly liver, is high in vitamins and minerals, but you can have too much of a good thing. Farm animals' liver is fine, but steer clear of polar bear liver. It contains poisonous levels of vitamin A: 50 times as much as beef liver. Eating it has killed Arctic explorers.

You can play with offal as well as eating it: inflated pigs' bladders make great balloons

▼ Trotter casserole

Pigs' trotters are a delicacy if they are well prepared. If the idea makes you feel queasy, remember that a foot is just a joint down from a knee, which you may have enjoyed as pork knuckle.

LET'S MAKE A TOUR of the many parts of a pig that you can eat but probably haven't.

At the very front, the pig's **snout** is a delicacy savoured especially in Spain; in Poland it's served up with soup.

The **ears** are a chewy delight: coated with breadcrumbs, they are deliciously crisp.

Lower down on the face, the **cheeks** are like fatty bacon. They are served as "Bath chaps" in Britain.

The **tongue** is rich meat and is delicious pressed like a ham and sliced.

Pork **brains** in milk gravy are popular served on scrambled egg in southern USA.

Moving on down, pig **guts** are traditionally filled with minced meat to make sausages. Today, only the best sausages are made from pig guts.

The **heart, kidneys** and **liver** can all be eaten, but some people find the flavour a little strong.

◄ The haggis

Scotland's haggis is an offal delight: a sheep's lungs, heart and liver stuffed inside its stomach for cooking. Home-made is best, but it's not easy to find the ingredients. Few butchers sell stomachs, and lungs are banned in the USA.

At the very end of the pig, the **tail** can be a tasty treat. You might see pigs' tails dyed pink and piled high on Afro-Caribbean market stalls.

Vampire Fare

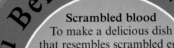
IN SCARY VAMPIRE stories, thirsty demons bite helpless victims and drink their blood. Vampires, who must drink human blood or die, exist only in story books. But the stories at least get one detail right: blood is a nourishing food.

◄ **Black pudding**
Blood by the pint may not sound tasty, but food made from blood can be. In the hungry past, butchers collected the blood of slaughtered animals. They mixed it with cream or oats and fat. Cooked in gut, the blood made a black sausage. You can still buy this today as black pudding. The town of Mortagne-au-Perche in Normandy, France, holds a *foire au boudin* (black pudding fair) every March. There is also an annual black pudding throwing event in Manchester, England.

When Italian traveller Marco Polo (1254–1324) visited China seven centuries ago, he marvelled at the country's Mongol warriors. "They will ride for ten days without taking a meal," he wrote. "They drink the blood of their horses. They open a vein and let the blood jet into their mouths."

◄ **Vlad the Impaler**
The vampire in Bram Stoker's (1847–1912) famous story *Dracula* is based on a European prince, Vlad Dracula (1431–1476). He was nicknamed "Vlad the Impaler" for his habit of impaling (spiking) his enemies on poles. Those who escaped spread terrible stories about him, leading to legends of blood-drinking. But Dracula is a hero in his native Romania and is remembered as cruel but fair.

Masai meals

Cattle are both food and money to the wandering Masai people of East Africa. When milk runs short, they mix it with blood drawn from their cows' veins.

A diet of blood ▲ ▶
Masai people eat almost nothing but beef, cow's blood and milk. They draw blood by firing an arrow at a cow's neck. They collect the blood in a gourd (hard-skinned fruit) or cup. The wound is plugged, and the cow's health is not affected. Neither is the health of the Masai. Though their diet is high in the fats that usually cause heart disease, the herbs they use in cooking keep them fit.

Most of us would draw the line at blood fresh from the vein, but as a soup, blood can be delicious. In Sweden, goose blood is the main ingredient for *Svartsoppa* (black soup), a traditional dish that's popular on St Martin's Eve (10 November). It tastes rather like rich gravy and it's not difficult to prepare – as long as you remember to add vinegar to the blood to stop it from clotting!

If blood turns you off, don't watch when your mum cooks a roast: that great gravy flavour comes from "pan juices" – blood in other words

23

You Dirty Rat!

F AR FROM BEING dirty, rats are "well tasted and wholesome meat, seeing that their food is entirely vegetable, and that they are clean, sleek and plump."

The Victorian author who wrote these words was trying to persuade his readers to eat a wider range of animals. With rodents, he bit off more than he could chew, because since Roman times, Europeans have never been keen on eating rats and mice. In other parts of the world people are not so choosy.

Barbecued rat ▲
Some small rodents can be eaten whole, barbecued and served with a dip. Grilled rat with baby onions was once a traditional dish in western France.

◄ Giant rat
The ultimate edible rat is the South American capybara, the world's largest rodent. It is 1.25 m (4 ft) long and can weigh as much as an adult woman. The capybara is raised for food on ranches in Venezuela. Its meat is very low in fat, and is usually eaten either dried or salted.

Meaty treats
In a field in India, some Irula people prepare to catch their dinner. They light straw in clay pots to make smoke. They blow this down holes in the ground to drive out field rats. Some of the rats end up in their cooking pots, along with rice the rats have hoarded underground.

If the Inuit catch several mice, they run a piece of twig through them and without stopping to skin them, they broil them over the fire

The flying mouse ▶
Bats are like mice with wings, and are just as edible – they are popular barbecued in Burma and Thailand. Fruit bats are a pest in parts of Northern Australia, where aboriginal people eat them grilled over hot coals. Don't be tempted to catch and eat bats yourself though. They are rare and protected in many places, and some can carry disease.

In ancient China, rats were called "household deer" and were a treat. Inuit people ate mice eagerly – spit roasted. Today, rodents make a welcome addition to the diet of many people who might otherwise never taste meat.

▼ Sleek and tasty
Field rats are not the scrawny beasts of city sewers. They are sleek, healthy, vegetarian – and tasty. Eating one is no odder than eating rabbits or hares, which also burrow in fields and destroy crops.

Extinction on a Plate

OUR GREED FOR FISH FILLETS and fingers may soon wipe out the ocean's fish, and some land animals face the same end. Unless we choose our food more carefully, we will eat some of the world's most wonderful creatures into extinction (none will remain alive).

Many fish are being battered to death in the deep-fat fryer. Cod, for example, was once so common that fishermen on Newfoundland's Grand Banks just lowered baskets into the water to catch the fish. Some were bigger than the men who caught them. Today, there are almost no cod left there.

◄ Kinder caviar
Caviar is the egg of the sturgeon fish, which is being wiped out by over-fishing. Each tiny egg you eat means one sturgeon fewer in the sea. An alternative to caviar is avruga – specially treated eggs of the common herring.

◄ Whale burger
Scientists in Japan say they kill whales only to study them – but Japanese people still eat whale meat. Japanese plans to kill more minke whales may destroy these graceful giants of the ocean.

Would You Believe...?

A heavy price
Beluga caviar is the most expensive food on Earth. One mouthful costs £20. The true price of this delicacy is higher still, because the number of sturgeon in the seas is declining. The Convention on International Trade in Endangered Species (CITES) has agreed strict limits on the catching of sturgeon.

Endangered on land

Hunting for food does not always put land animals and birds in danger of extinction. Unfortunately though, hunters are not the only threat to the world's rare wildlife. Other human activities, such as cutting down forest trees, also threaten rare creatures; hunting just finishes the job.

▲ Dead as a dodo
Huge, clumsy and unable to fly, dodos once thrived on Mauritius – until Dutch sailors discovered this Indian Ocean island in about 1600. The birds had no fear of people, so they were easy to catch and cook. Within 75 years, the dodo was extinct.

◄ Bushmeat
Chimpanzees in West Africa may be extinct within 40 to 50 years. The illegal hunting and eating of apes, known as the "bushmeat crisis" is having a great effect on the rate of decline of this creature. Deforestation, human encroachment and disease are also contributing.

◄ Mammoth menu
Over-hunting helped to kill off the mega-fauna (giant beasts) of the Stone Age. If our ancestors had known a bit more about conservation, we might still be eating mammoth steaks to this day.

Farming won't save **wild fish from extinction: to produce 1 kg (2.2 lb) of farmed fish, it takes 4 kg (8.8 lb) of** fishmeal – made from wild fish

Mud Pudding

EVERYONE ENJOYS MAKING mud pies when they are kids. A few of us just never grow out of the habit. Some people eat mud just because they like the taste of it. Others say it makes them feel good. In some areas, women who are pregnant (expecting babies) are keen on eating mud.

Mud fans are choosy about where it comes from. They dig mud from deep below the ground where the soil is safer to eat. In Africa, earth from termite hills is a popular choice; it's sold in city market stalls.

Eating a little mud may help children to develop the ability to fight off disease

Keeping hunger away

In times of famine, more people get a taste for mud. When German and Austrian miners of the early 20th century could not afford butter or flour, they replaced them with earth and clay.

◀ Why do young kids eat dirt?
It's no use asking them. They will just stare at you as if the answer is obvious. Scientists have estimated that even children who eat dirt accidentally – on food they have dropped on the ground, or by sucking dirty fingers – swallow up to a teaspoonful a week.

Eating the church

The stone walls of some European churches are marked with cup-shaped hollows. Superstitious people carved them, seeking a cure for the diseases they suffered. They believed that since churches were holy places, eating dust scraped from their walls would heal them.

▼ Acorns and mud gravy
Native American people from California used to collect acorns that contained poisons called tannic acids. Mixing the powdered acorns with clay removed three-quarters of the poisons, making them safe to eat.

Birds and beasts do it too ▶
Animals such as this South American macaw have an instinct for eating soils that are rich in useful minerals. Places where these soils occur are famous for the animals they attract. The town of French Lick in Southern Indiana, USA, grew up around a mineral lick that animals used.

Useful minerals

Some muds contain minerals such as magnesium, iron and zinc. These are missing from the diet of some people. Mud can also help remove natural poisons from plants, making them safe to eat.

● ● ● ● ● ● ● ● ● ● ● ● ● ● ● ● ● ● ● ●

Eating mud might seem mad, but there are good reasons to do it. Clay settles and calms upset stomachs. You may have even eaten some yourself. A popular remedy sold by pharmacies contains kaolin – white clay. But just because some mud is sometimes good for some people, not all mud is good for everyone. Dirt often contains poisons and other unhealthy things, so don't eat it yourself.

Snappy Snacks

Cancer cure ▶
In Guatemala, there once was a belief that eating a live lizard cured cancer. Scientists visited the town of Amatitlan in 1780 to look into the claim, but there is no record of their research.

S LITHERING, SCALY, SLIMY or just plain dangerous, amphibians and reptiles are not a popular choice for dinner. But frogs, lizards, turtles, snakes and crocodiles are no strangers to the cooking pot. They were once an important part of the diet everywhere in the world. In Asia and South America, people still eat them with gusto.

Turtles used to be a common delicacy on European tables. Salty sailors in the Caribbean feasted on them. So what put us off? Perhaps it's what they look like. Some reptiles have fearsome faces. And compared to fur and feather, a scaly, horny or slippery skin seems unnatural. It doesn't make the meat less tasty though.

Fewer frogs
Killing frogs for their legs has made them scarce, allowing insects that frogs eat to multiply in number, threatening crops. So if a waiter offers you frogs' legs, tell him to "hop it!"

A taste for frogs' legs earned the French a rude national nickname

◀ **Iguanas**
Never as popular as turtles because of their looks, iguanas are actually quite tasty. They have tender white flesh and their fat is a delicacy. However, according to one diner, "when one of its paws happens to stick up in the dish, it reminds one too much of the alligator to eat it with any great relish."

◄ Gators on a plate
Alligators reared for the table are not endangered, and the meat is low in cholesterol so it's healthy to eat. Each year, American farmers raise 220,000 alligators in Florida and Louisiana, where most of the ranches are based.

Rattlesnake and alligator steaks are on a few menus in the American West. But most of us would still snap "No!" to a crocodile sandwich. It's probably a good thing too. Our ancestors' taste for roast tortoise and turtle almost wiped out some species.

Would You Believe...? Would You Believe...?

Turtles
Tortoises and turtles became popular dishes among wealthy Londoners in the 18th century. When a pub served a giant turtle in 1753, a wall of the brick oven had to be removed to fit it inside. By the 19th century, Britain was importing 15,000 of the beasts a year, some weighing more than 150 kg (330 lb).

Snake steaks ▼
A snake is a good food source, especially in deserts, where other game is scarce. Kalahari bushmen are preparing this snake for the table, but you can also find snake in restaurants from Kansas to Texas, USA, where "Rattler Roundups" are a tourist attraction.

▼ **Crunchy critters**
Deep-fried grasshoppers make a tasty, crunchy snack! Mmmmmm.

A Diet
of Insects

HOW MANY INSECTS did you eat today? More than you imagine! There are fly eggs in fruit juice, maggots in pizza sauce and insect parts in peanut butter. Food safety laws recognise that it isn't possible to remove all insects from food. They allow six insect parts per 20 g (0.7 oz) portion of peanut butter.

There is nothing wrong with eating insects. In fact they make very good food. In parts of southern Africa, insects supply people with two-thirds of the protein they need, and in Southeast Asia, insects are a favourite street snack.

Anyone for locusts?

These large grasshoppers eat whole fields of crops – but we can get our own back by eating them! Just remove the wings and back legs and boil until soft (about half an hour). Then stir-fry in sesame oil with garlic and chilli. Sprinkle with soy sauce and serve with salad and crusty bread.

▲ **Yes please!**
This American schoolgirl is trying a fried cricket as part of a project called "Global Kitchen".

People eat insect dishes because they are traditional **and** delicious

Leggy lunch ▶
Strictly speaking, spiders are not insects but, like other creepy crawlies, they can make excellent snacks. Spiders were first eaten in Cambodia due to food shortages, but they are now a delicacy.

Other creepy crawlies

Crickets, grasshoppers and locusts all belong to the same animal family, but they are not the only creepy crawlies that can be used to make a meal. Spiders, dragonflies and worms can be found on the menu too.

▲ Flying food

On the island of Bali in Southeast Asia, hunting dragonflies is an enjoyable sport – with a tasty bonus. The insects are very hard to catch so hunters coat the tips of "whippy sticks" with sticky tree sap to trap the dragonflies. Then they wrap the dragonflies up in a banana leaf and grill them.

TODAY'S MENU

Starters

Creepy crawlies are ideal for snacks and starters. You don't need a knife and fork – just pick them up in your fingers! Most insects have a tasty texture contrast. The outer shell is deliciously crunchy. The inside is moist, soft and often creamy or sweet.

Scorpion snack
Cooking takes the sting out of its tail!

Thai sour ant eggs
Biting bursts the thin skin, releasing a soft, cheesy centre.

Main courses

Insects make a perfect ingredient for a satisfying, healthy main meal. Maggots, for example, contain three times as much protein as best beef. Insects are also an ideal diet food. Grasshoppers in particular are very low in fat.

Diving beetle
Deep fry, but remember to pull off the wings before eating.

Moth cakes
Singe off legs and wings, grind to a fine powder, mix to a paste with water and bake.

Desserts

Why stop at savoury foods? There's no reason why you can't eat insect sweets as well! Some, such as the honey ant, would never have got their name if people did not know they were tasty and sweet to eat. Other insect desserts need help from sugar and chocolate.

Cricket lolly
Clear sugar on a stick shows off the treat trapped inside.

Choc grubs
Lightly cook grubs, dry carefully and dip in chocolate for a sweet treat.

Think I'll go and eat Worms

NEED TO LOSE WEIGHT? WHAT about a meal that is no more fattening than best beef, but has three times the goodness. This brilliant diet food is the humble maggot. Maggots are insects in disguise. Like the insects they turn into, maggots are members of a group of animals called invertebrates – creatures without backbones.

Slipping down ▶
Most people find that land slugs are too disgusting to eat. Sea slugs, on the other hand, seem to slip down quite easily. Known as sea cucumbers, they are so popular in Chinese restaurants that some species are now endangered.

This group also includes worms, snails and slugs. All these beasts are edible, but only the snail has ever made it to posh dinner tables. Worms and slugs seem to have been less popular.

• • • • • • • • • •

The popularity of snails for food led to "snail rustling" in Britain in 2005

Would You Believe...?

Snails
As *escargots*, snails are a popular dish in France. Feeding them on lettuce leaves for four days cleans dirt from their guts, and soaking them in salt and vinegar gets rid of the slime. Then it's just a matter of boiling and baking with garlic butter. But don't eat snails from the garden. They may contain poisons.

◀ Silkworm kebab
The fine threads that are woven into silk clothes come from silkworms – the grubs of a large moth. The grubs spin the thread to make cocoons in which they turn into moths. The workers who unwind the thread get a tasty bonus at the end, for the grubs are delicious. Because so many countries produce silk, there are lots of recipes: the grubs are good boiled, fried, roasted, baked, steamed or, as here, barbecued on skewers.

Mopane worms ▶
The grubs of the emperor moth are eaten in Botswana, Zimbabwe and parts of South Africa. Called mopane worms, the caterpillars are boiled or fried after the cook has squeezed out the contents of the gut.

Grub's up

Most insects pass through a larval stage between egg and flying critter forms. For hungry people, the larvae, also called grubs or maggots, have several advantages. They are easy to catch, many have a high food value and they don't have lots of bits to get stuck between your teeth.

To get used to the idea of putting a maggot in your mouth, talk to anglers. They use live maggots on their hooks. In winter they warm them in their mouths to make them wriggle. It's a small step to chewing and swallowing. Good cooking, of course, turns them from a snack into a meal.

Witchetty grubs ▶
Native Australian people find witchetty grubs in the roots of the acacia – the witchetty bush. Ten large grubs provide an adult with enough protein for a day. They are eaten raw or roasted in the dying embers of a fire.

Dicing with Death

▲ Dangerous nuts
Cycad nuts are a traditional food source for Australian Aborigines. The nuts look delicious, but they are poisonous unless they are prepared properly. To make them edible, cooks crack open the shells, pound the nuts inside to a paste, soak or wash the paste in water, then make it into bread.

OUTSIDE A HUNDRED restaurants in the Japanese city of Tokyo hang strange lanterns. They are made from the inflated skins of blowfish. These signs show that the restaurants serve blowfish, or *fugu*, a luxury *sushi* (raw fish) dish. It is not the flavour of *fugu* that makes it special: it doesn't taste of much. The attraction is that the blowfish contains a deadly poison.

There's enough poison in one *fugu* fish to kill 30 people – and 20 Japanese people die each year from eating it

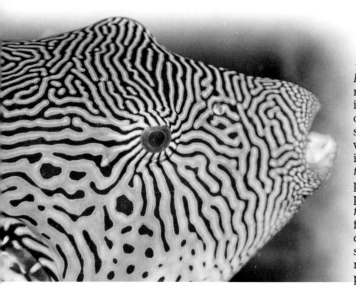

◄ Blowfish blowout
Fugu is one of the most expensive fish in Japan, so people order it is a way of showing off their wealth. The danger involved in eating *fugu* also makes it popular. Most people killed by *fugu* prepared the fish at home: they did not have the skill needed to remove all the poisonous parts.

Eating *fugu* is more like a dare than a dinner. Only careful preparation from a trained chef saves diners from a swift death. But people eat other poisonous foods for sensible reasons – such as nourishment. For example, manioc is the main food of 600 million people around the world, but it contains a strong poison called cyanide.

◀ **Don't eat your greens**
Some "greens" should not be eaten! Rhubarb leaves contain oxalic acid which can damage your kidneys if you eat it. And all parts of the potato plant except the root contain poison, and even this can make you ill if it has turned green.

Would You Believe...? Would You Believe...? Would You Believe...?

Deadly decoration
Marzipan in sweets and cake decorations contains the poison cyanide. This comes from the bitter almonds that are used to flavour the paste. Marzipan is one of the few foods for which there are permitted levels of cyanide, but you would have to eat an awful lot of it to get sick.

Also called cassava, manioc is made from a starchy plant root. But you can't just cook and eat the root. Just a slice or two would kill you. It has to be prepared by grating and straining to squeeze out the poison. It can be processed into tapioca, a familiar pudding. Countless other foods contain poison in small amounts. Some of them are very popular.

Stone fruit ▲
The stones of apricots, plums and cherries, and the seeds of apples contain cyanide. Just 15 apricot kernels (the soft centre inside the stone) are enough to kill a child. Fortunately, the kernel is hard to remove.

Incredible
Inedibles

DON'T TRY THIS AT HOME! Risking indigestion and injury, people eat the most unlikely things. Sword-swallowers and fire-eaters sound the worst, but they don't actually eat anything – the long blades come straight back out, and the flames never go down in the first place. Others make a meal of money, pebbles, cutlery and almost anything else they can fit in their mouths.

Some people have forced down objects to hide them – swallowing coins rather than give them up to robbers. Others have a mental illness called pica and can't resist eating strange things. But most people who swap meat and greens for metal and glass do so for money.

A sharp appetite ▲
Expert sword-swallowers can swallow a 62 cm (2 ft) blade. Sliding it down brings the mouth, throat and stomach into a straight line. They train themselves not to choke, and the blunt sword does the rest.

Eating everything
Doctors call the ability to eat non-food items "polyphagia". Their studies have shown that although smaller objects soon pass through, bigger ones stay in the gut and cause injuries.

It can be dangerous just to watch someone eat fire

◄ **Fire-eaters**
Touching torches on their tongues, fire-eaters risk burns, but they don't actually eat fire. A coating of saliva protects their mouths against the flames. People have to go to fire-eating classes to learn how to perform this dangerous trick.

Hearty eater ▲
Frenchman Michel Lotito eats TV sets, supermarket trolleys and bicycles. He took two years to eat a light aircraft. "Monsieur Mangetout" (Mr Eatall) can eat so much metal because his stomach lining is twice the normal thickness.

As early as the 18th century, entertainers ate stones to draw crowds. One advertised that "…after the stones are swallowed they may be heard to clink in the belly the same as in a pocket!" Not to be outdone, his hungry rivals ate knives, forks, spoons and broken glass.

▼ **Gut reaction**
If you are still hungry at the end of a meal, don't eat the cutlery. X-ray photographs of people who eat metal objects show where they end up. X-rays have also proved that sword-swallowers are not conjurers: they really do put the blades down their throats.

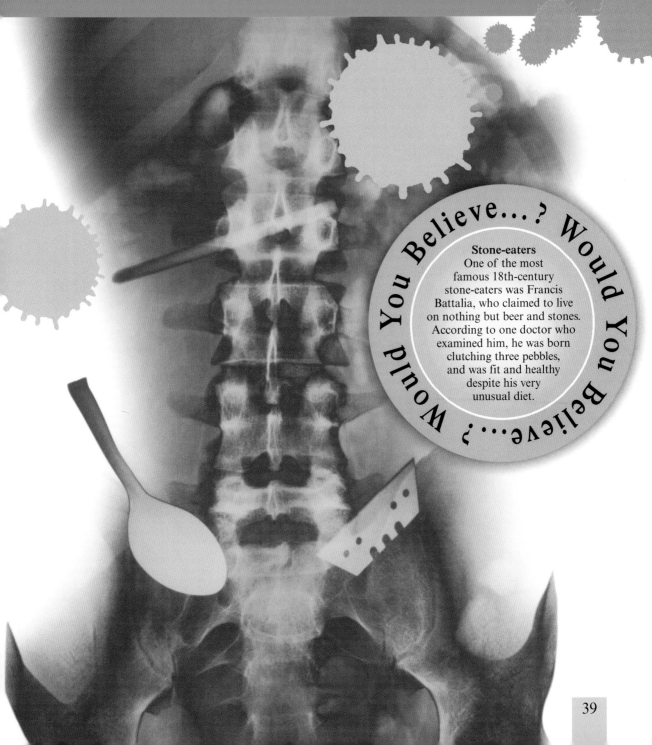

Would You Believe…?

Stone-eaters
One of the most famous 18th-century stone-eaters was Francis Battalia, who claimed to live on nothing but beer and stones. According to one doctor who examined him, he was born clutching three pebbles, and was fit and healthy despite his very unusual diet.

Farms or Factories?

T HE FOOD WE EAT EVERY DAY tastes great, but what's actually in it? You can find some answers if you read the boxes and bags, but labels don't tell you everything. For instance, cheap pies, burgers and sausages often contain something called "mechanically recovered meat", or MRM. It's a kind of watery paste made by scraping or washing left-over meat from bones.

Meat is not the only food product that hides unpleasant secrets. Other processed foods are flavoured with chemicals. That delicious pie you ate last week, for example, tasted really strongly of apple. However, its flavour probably came from a chemical called Ethyl-2-methyl butyrate.

Chemical traces ▲
Even real fruit can contain traces of the chemicals sprayed on it to keep bugs off. Little of it contains enough to harm you though.

Factory farming
As supermarkets pay less and less for the food they sell us, some farmers take dangerous shortcuts to keep profits up. In crowded fields and sheds, diseases spread rapidly between stressed animals.

◄ Chicken run
Even in the cleanest chicken processing factories, the gut contents of some birds spills on to the meat. This spreads a germ called campylobacter on about half of all chickens. Careful cooking kills the germs, making the meat safe. But if the meat is not cooked properly, anyone eating it gets a stomach upset – if they are lucky. The unlucky ones die.

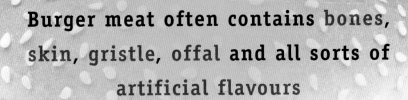

Burger meat often contains bones, skin, gristle, offal and all sorts of artificial flavours

Fast food ▲
Even "pure beef" hamburgers may have been made from the meat of cattle that were fed blood, or newspaper and sawdust from poultry-shed floors. (Beef cattle are naturally vegetarians and should eat only grass and grain.)

There are good reasons why the food we eat is not all it seems to be. If farmers did not spray crops, food would cost more and fruit and vegetables would look less perfect. And if food processors did not add chemicals, food would not keep so well. If we want purer food, we will all need to pay a little more, shop more often and put up with odd-shaped carrots.

Fads and Fasts

Fasting and de-tox ▶
There have been so many crazy diets, it's hard to sort out truth from fiction. Eating just orange-coloured foods, having a spoonful of ice-cream every two hours and drinking lots of iced water have all been suggested as ways to lose weight. Or how about eating only foods that begin with the letter C?

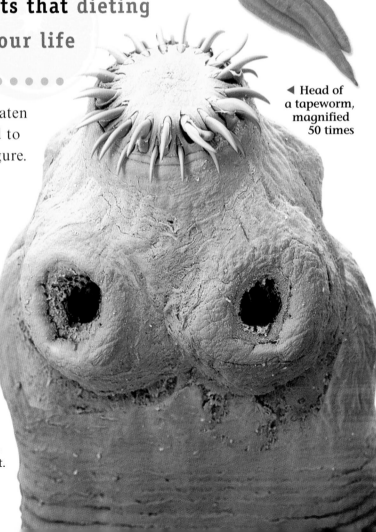

D IETING REALLY BEGAN ABOUT 150 years ago, when London coffin-maker William Banting (1797–1878) grew so fat that he had to walk downstairs backwards. On his doctor's advice, he cut out sugar and starch and lost 23 kg (3.6 stone). He then wrote the world's first diet book.

If you are only a little overweight, some research suggests that dieting can shorten your life

Since Banting, fat people have eaten ever-crazier diets, and even tried to starve their way to a slimmer figure. But as any dieter will tell you, nothing seems to work for long. Scientists now know that eating less can actually make people fatter. Their bodies get used to less food, so when the diet ends they pile on the pounds again.

◀ Head of a tapeworm, magnified 50 times

Eating worms ▶
In the 1950s, opera star Maria Callas (1923–1977) lost 28 kg (62 lbs) in a year allegedly after swallowing a tapeworm, which grew in her gut. Diet pills holding tapeworm eggs were on sale in the USA at the time, but she may have picked up the parasite by eating undercooked meat.

A Light Repast

Fasting

Starvation diets are a fashionable way to get thin and "de-tox". But going without food robs the body of energy, making it hard for the organs to work properly. Waste products stay inside the body for longer, and you get headaches and bad breath. Fasting for more than a day is dangerous for young people and those with diabetes or heart disease.

▲ **Diet food and drinks**
Patent weight-reducing foods promise to make dieting quick and easy. But products such as Allen and Hanbury's 1905 Diet Health Drink – "just mix with hot water" – were expensive to buy and boring to eat. Few people who ate them would have got any thinner.

At least one-quarter of us diet, and there are nearly 13,000 different diet books to tell us how to do it. Many of them outline fad diets that won't help readers. Some recommend dangerous diets. We buy them because we want an easy way to get thin. Sadly, there is no easy way, but there is a simple way. Anyone can lose weight by exercising more and eating less. The catch is that you must do this all your life, not just for a few weeks.

In the 17th century, only the wealthy could afford to eat well, so it was not fashionable to be skinny – women in paintings of that time look fat to us

What's so Weird about That?

PERHAPS YOU HAVE SMILED or gasped, or felt slightly sick as you read this book. These are perfectly natural reactions, but don't be too quick to laugh at other people's meals. Often, their strange dishes are as nourishing as anything you eat. And they might find your diet as disgusting as you find theirs.

In many parts of Asia, for example, nobody drinks or cooks with milk. Vietnamese people find cheese, butter, milk and cream as horrible as we might find stir-fried grasshoppers.

Would You Believe...? Would You Believe...?

Scary supper
Strange new foods take a while to get used to. When a new food plant was brought to Europe in the 16th century, few people liked it, and 200 years passed before many farmers grew it. Even in 1770 people in Germany preferred to starve rather than eat it. What was it? The potato!

◄ **Roast ram**
In parts of Mongolia, roasted sheep's head is served up on special occasions. The cheeks and eyeballs are considered a delicacy and are offered to the guest of honour.

Yucky or yummy?
Even if nothing you have read makes you hungry, maybe you will think twice before turning up your nose at a strange dish. Whether we say "Yuck" or "Yum" depends on what we are used to eating. Remember, if something swims, flies, crawls or walks, somebody somewhere is probably eating it right now!

Those who refuse to try anything new might escape poisoning but die of boredom

Find out More

You can find out lots more about strange and surprising foods from these websites and places to visit.

Websites

Weird foods
http://www.foodmuseum.com
The Food Museum is an interesting site about food in all its variety, with lots of information on everything from school dinners to frogs' legs, famine and chewy squid suppers.

Prehistoric cooking
http://www.channel4.com/history/timeteam/snapshot_cooking.html
Channel 4's Time Team page on Stone Age food, with a link to a page of prehistoric recipes.

Roman recipes
http://www.romans-in-britain.org.uk/arl_roman_cooking-pt1.htm
A couple of pages about Roman cooking in Britain – find out how the Romans cooked, preserved and ate their food.

Blood on the menu
http://www.bbc.co.uk/food/recipes/mostof_blackpudding.shtml
A BBC page about the history of black pudding around Europe and how it is made.

Dead as a dodo
http://www.oum.ox.ac.uk/dodo.htm
The Oxford University Museum of Natural History's dodo page – find out what the dodo really looked like.

Bugs on the plate
http://news.nationalgeographic.com/kids/2004/04/eatingbugs.html
A National Geographic page on eating insects – could you eat a cricket lollipop?

Eating worms
http://www.frenchgourmetstore.com/escargot.php
A site where you can buy oven-ready snails.

Places to visit

Hampton Court Tudor Kitchens
Hampton Court Palace
East Molesey
Surrey KT8 9AU
Telephone: 0870 753 7777
Website: http://www.historicroyalpalaces.org/webcode/content.asp?ID=411
Visit the kitchens of one of Britain's most famous royal palaces. The kitchens are set up as they would have been on Midsummer's Day, 1542, for the Feast of John the Baptist. You can follow a dish from raw ingredients to the king's table.

Cadbury World
Linden Road
Bournville
Birmingham B30 2LU
Telephone (automated ticket line): 0121 451 4180
Website: http://www.cadburyworld.co.uk/en/cworld
A visit to the world of chocolate begins in the "Aztec forest" where you can learn how Europeans found out about chocolate from the Aztec people.

Visit an organic farm
To find out about sustainable farming, and how it improves the food we eat, you can visit an organic farm. You will be able to: walk a farm trail and enjoy the countryside and its wildlife; stock up with the freshest food at the farm shop; taste the produce at farm cafés and enjoy special open days or even stay on a farm. You can find your nearest farm at the Soil Association website: http://www.soilassociation.org/farmvisits

Historic cookery demonstrations
Gary Waidson regularly demonstrates cooking from the Stone Age to the early medieval period. He has run events at National Trust properties, and can visit schools.
17 Chatsworth Close
Shaw, Oldham
Lancashire OL2 8EB
Telephone: 01706 671282
Website: http://www.lore-and-saga.co.uk

Glossary

Many of the food terms used in this book are explained on this page. Where a word is in italics, it means the word has its own entry.

banquet
Very large and grand feast.

black pudding
Kind of sausage filled with blood and other delicious ingredients.

bushmeat
Any forest animal other than *game* that is hunted for food.

cannibalism
Eating an animal of the same kind, eg. humans eating humans.

caviar
Eggs of the sturgeon, a fish that is close to extinction.

cholesterol
Natural body chemical that makes fat clog up the arteries, causing heart disease.

de-tox diet
Not eating certain, or all, food, in the belief that this will flush poisons from the body.

diabetes
Too much sugar in the blood. Gaining weight and a bad *diet* can cause this serious disease.

diet
What someone eats and drinks; also short for weight-reducing diet.

digestion
Breaking down of food in the gut, so that the body can use it for growth and *energy*.

energy
The body's ability to do work.

famine
Widespread hunger when food runs out.

fasting
Deliberately not eating when there is plenty of food available.

fugu
A kind of fish, eaten in Japan, that has poisonous organs.

game
Any wild animal traditionally hunted for food.

gristle
Tough tissue that helps hold together an animal's body.

haggis
Scots dish made from *offal* boiled in a sheep's stomach.

indigestion
Bloated feeling that comes from eating too much or too quickly.

kosher
A Hebrew word for food that is fit to eat and follows Jewish *diet* laws.

Mechanically Recovered Meat
Shreds of meat squeezed from bones for cheap meat products.

mineral
Chemical needed for health and found in foods.

nourishment
That part of food that is good for us, keeping our bodies growing.

offal
Parts of a food animal that are not muscle, especially organs.

processed food
Food that is sold partly or fully prepared for eating.

protein
Substance in food that our bodies need for growth and to repair damage.

savoury
Not sweet; often *spicy* or salty.

shellfish
Sea creatures that have their skeletons outside their bodies, such as oysters and lobsters.

spice
Strongly flavoured tropical plant used in cooking.

starch
Substance in fruits, roots and seeds that provides *energy* when eaten.

sushi
Japanese dish of raw fish.

tortilla
Thin flat bread made from corn.

vegetarian
Someone who does not eat meat or fish.

vitamin
An organic (carbon-containing) chemical found in food, and needed in small quantities as part of a healthy *diet*.

Index

Picture credits

The publisher would like to thank the following for their kind permission to reproduce their photographs:

Position key: c=centre; b=bottom; l=left; r=right; t=top

Cover: Front: tr: Peter Menzel/Science Photo Library; cr: © Big Cheese Photo LLC/Alamy; bl: Mary Evans/Explorer Archives; tl: The Natural History Museum/Alamy. Back: bl: OUP/Photodisc.

1: C. Schmidt/Zeta/Corbis; 4r: Viennareport Agency/Corbis/Sygma; 4bl: Darren Sawyer/Bookwork; 5cr: NHPA/David Middleton; 6br: NHPA/Ernie Janes; 7b: Richard Platt; 7tl: Archivo Iconografico, SA/ Corbis; 8tl: British Museum/Heritage Image Partnership; 9t: Gianni Dagli Orti/Corbis; 10br: Ann Ronan Picture Library/Heritage Image Partnership; 11c: Werner Forman/Corbis; 11tl, 11r: Darren Sawyer/ Bookwork; 12bl: Corbis; 12c; 12br: James L Amos/Corbis; 13tr: Topfoto/Werner Archive; 14cl: Bettman/Corbis; 14–15b: Bookwork; 15tr: Edifice/Corbis; 16–17t: Photocuisine/Corbis; 17cr: Charles & Josette Lenars/Corbis; 18 tl: NHPA/Martin Harvey; 18b: Academy of Natural Sciences of Philadelphia/Corbis;

19tr: Warren Photographic; 20cl: Poodles Rock/Corbis; 20tr: Darren Sawyer/ Bookwork; 21c: Rougemont Maurice/Corbis/ Sygma; 21tr: Darren Sawyer/ Bookwork; 21bl: Darren Sawyer/ Bookwork; 22c: Darren Sawyer/ Bookwork; 22bl: Mary Evans Picture Library; 23t; 23cr: Joe Mcdonald/ Corbis; 24tr: Darren Sawyer/ Bookwork; 24cl: NHPA/James Warwick; 25tr: Reuters/Corbis; 25c: Darren Sawyer/Bookwork; 25b: Michael Freeman; 26bl: Lucky Pierrot/ Handout/Reuters/Corbis; 26tr: Darren Sawyer/ Bookwork; 27tr: DK Ltd/ Corbis; 28l: Gerhard Steiner/Corbis; 28tr: NHPA/George Bernard; 29r: NHPA/Martin Harvey; 30bl: NHPA/ Martin Wendler; 31tl: US Fish and Wildlife Service; 31b: Anthony Bannister/Corbis/ Gallow Images; 32tl: Michael Freeman/Corbis; 32bl: Mike Segar/ Reuters/Corbis; 33c: Reuters/Corbis; 34cl: NHPA/Ant Photo Library; 35tl: Keren Su/Corbis; 35cr: Anthony Bannister/Gallow Images/Corbis; 35br: NHPA/John Shaw; 36bl: FLPA/ Norbert Wu/ Minden Pictures; 36tr: Penny Tweedie/ Corbis; 37tl: Spencer Jones/ Picture Arts/Corbis; 37c: Darren Sawyer/ Bookwork; 38tr: Hulton-Deutsch Collection; 38bl: Pablo Corral V/Corbis; 39: SPL; 40bl: China Photo/Reuters/ Corbis; 40tr: David Pollack/Corbis; 41tr: Envision/ Corbis; 42tr: Douglas Kirkland/Corbis; 42cr: Darren Sawyer/Bookwork; 42br: Eye of Science/ SPL; 43tr: Mary Evans Picture Library; 44bl: Hamid Sardar/Corbis.